THIS IS TAP

THIS IS TAP

SAVION GLOVER FINDS HIS FUNK

BY Selene Castrovilla

ILLUSTRATED BY
Laura Freeman

HOLIDAY HOUSE · NEW YORK

Livity, givity, lovity, dovity,

BRING,
BRING,
BRING!

4

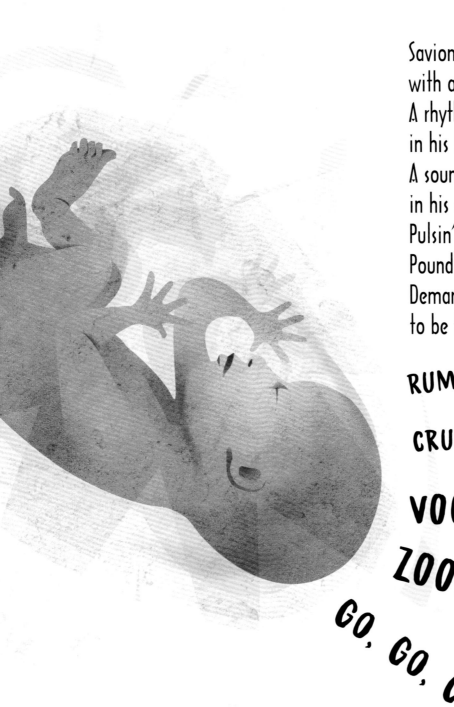

Savion Glover was born
with a beat
A rhythm
in his head
A sound
in his soul
Pulsin'
Poundin'
Demandin'
to be free

RUMBLY,

CRUMBLY,

VOOMITY,

ZOOMITY,

GO, GO, GO!

Even in the womb
he was movin'
to 'da beat
side to side
'cross Mommy's belly
kickin'
to the tempo
of her typin'

CLICKITY, TICKETY, CLACKITY, FRACKITY, KICK, KICK, KICK!

Mommy knew this baby
was gonna be
different
Third son
to join her fam-fam
So tired,
she asked God,
"Please help
with his name."
Letters appeared
on a chalkboard
in her mind

SCRIBBILY, BIBBILY, SCRAWLITY, SPRAWLITY,
PRAY, PRAY, PRAY!

They spelled "Savior!"
She shifted the "r" to an "n"

Came time to be
walkin´,
her Savion
had no flat feet!

Up from a crawl,

to the knuckles
of his toes

10

Vaultin'
through the house,
a human
pogo stick!

BINGITY,
FLINGITY,
BOINGITY,
ZOINGITY,

BOUNCE,
BOUNCE,
BOUNCE!

11

Poundin' out
'da beat
on anythin'
he found

Pots,
pans,
a colander,

even his head
'gainst the walls

CLINKITY, TINKITY,

BAM,

BAM,

BAM!

CLANGITY,

BANGITY,

13

Age four
he started drum class,
amazin'
teachers
with 'da beat!
Happy to be
groovin'
to the sound
of his sticks

HITTITY, PITTITY, TATTITY, RATTITY,

DRUM, DRUM, DRUM!

14

All this rhythm,
why not put him in dance?
That's what Mommy did
Seven years old,
he slipped on those shoes

Soul
meets
sole
From that day on,
Savion danced
All the time
Not practicin'
Livin'

TIPPITY, FLIPPITY,

TAPPITY, FLAPPITY,

TROMP, TROMP, TROMP!

15

Other people saw places,
Savion
HEARD them
Each scene grooved
to its own pace
Tap pulsed
everywhere,
in every thing
He felt it
thumpin'
in his head,

he felt it
throbbin'
in his feet

At the lockers
In the street
On the bus

CRAMMITY,

SLAMMITY,

JINGITY,

DINGITY,

VROOM, **VROOM, VROOM!**

Broadway bound
at ten
Folks linin' up
for a peek
at those feet's
incredible
feats
Then to Paris,
another show
A movie,
TV too

WHISKITY, FRISKITY,

SWOOSHITY, WHOOSHITY, UP, UP, UP!

What Savion loved most
was hoofin'
with the old-time
cats in Harlem,
tap masters
who called him
"The Sponge"
They taught him
'bout hittin'

SHOOPITY, DOOPITY, SHUFFILY, BUFFILY,

HIT, HIT, HIT!

19

Hittin' meant
expressin'
yourself
with your feet
Makin'
a statement
When the audience
picked up
on what you were
puttin' down,
you hit

RIFFITY,

SPIFFITY,

BOMPITY,

ROMPITY,

CLAP,

CLAP,

CLAP!

20

But tap
was old school
A dinosaur,
they said
Jazz was
out,
hip-hop
in
Top o' that,
Savion felt restless
Tired of the
same steps
He'd danced enough
to others' beats
Time to
BE his own

THINKITY,
LINKITY,
DIGGITY,
BIGGITY,

CLICK,
CLICK,
CLICK!

21

Mixin' it up
in a hip-hop club,
Savion found
his groove
'Da beat
swirled through him,
boppin' round his body
like a challenge
to be met
Only one choice:
let it loose
His feet hammered out
those feelin's inside:

BOOM, BOOM, BOOM!

BAH, BUH,

BOOM, BOOM, BOOM,

The crowd was
down
with it, man
This cat was bringin'
`da funk!
Now Savion knew:
blend the old
with the new!
He would
respect the past
while definin' the moment
Tap meets
hip-hop

TIGGITY, SWIGGITY,

TAGGITY, BAGGITY,

SWEET,

SWEET,

SWEET!

It hit him like
lightnin':
Time 'ta spread the word!
Create a show,
share
'da funk
Bring in
'da noise!

ZAPPITY, BAPPITY, BIPPITY, ZIPPITY, VOLT, VOLT, VOLT!

24

'Da noise meant
excellence,
puttin' down
the best he had
Dancin'
'cross history,
tracin' racism
through tap
Savion's role?
'Da Beat!

TRACKITY, PACKITY,
TRAMPITY, STAMPITY,
POUND, POUND, POUND!

25

Opening night
Back on Broadway
Electric wave
sizzlin'
through the crowd
Audience
buzzin'
with chitchat:
"What's this cat Savion up to?"
No shufflin'
off to Buffalo,
no top hat and tails
This was tap
raw
This was tap with
attitude
This was HIS tap

FUNKITY, SPUNKITY, JUMPITY, THUMPITY, POW, POW, POW!

Man, he was hittin' tonight!
Savion heard the voices
cheerin'
past the lights,
but mostly he dug
the sound of his feet
slammin'
the stage
No nerves,
no fear
Just satisfaction

GROOVITY, MOVITY, SHUCKITY, PLUCKITY, RUSH, RUSH, RUSH!

From the audience,
Mommy cheered
This was it
Destiny
Becomin' all he was
meant to be

TRIPPITY, HIPPITY, JAMMITY,

WHAMMITY, FREE, FREE, FREE!

Sweat dripped down
his forehead
He smelled it,
soakin'
through his shirt
He was givin' birth
right there on stage,
to himself as an artist
All he'd ever learned,
discovered,
created
It poured out of him:
blended, shaken, stirred

WHIFFITY, SNIFFITY, SWIRLITY, WHIRLITY,

BURST, BURST, BURST!

'DA BEAT
Tap beat
through history
It beat through
his veins,
onto the stage
He and tap
were one
'Da beat goes on

SCRAPPITY,

STRAPPITY,

SCRUFFITY,

SCUFFITY,

STOMP,

STOMP,

STOMP!

The crowd clamored:
More!
Fuel for his feet
People said he hoofed faster
than anyone they'd seen,
in warp speed
They tagged him a genius
The "savior of tap"
Naw, he was just
puttin'
down the rhythms
rattlin'
through his head

RIPPITY,
DIPPITY,
CHUGGITY,
TUGGITY,
BLAST,
BLAST,
BLAST!

31

Savion's feet thundered on the stage
like a set of ragin' drums
All the percussion
packed
into two black shoes
Bass
Tom-tom
Snare
Hi-hat
Cymbals
The sounds shook through his body,
explodin'
through his soul like
fireworks
on the fourth
Sweet, man

CRACKITY, STACKITY, POPPITY, BOPPITY, CRASH, CRASH, CRASH!

Translation:
Wake up world! This is tap!

RHYTHM.
HITTIN'.
NOISE.
FUNK.

THIS IS TAP.

AFTERWORD

RIGHT from his entrance into the world on November 19, 1973, Savion Glover moved to his own beat.

Savion drew sound from everything he could grab hold of. He even used himself to make rhythm, bouncing through his family's Newark, New Jersey house on the knuckles of his toes as soon as he could walk.

At age four, Savion started drum lessons. With those tempos banging through his head, he was a natural.

At age seven, he strode into dance class at the Broadway Dance Center in Manhattan.

He came out tapping.

From that moment, for every moment since, rhythm erupted from Savion's feet.

At ten, Savion was cast in the title role of Broadway's *The Tap Dance Kid*. Officially in "show biz," he transferred from a Catholic school in Newark to the Professional Children's School in Manhattan (a year later he moved to the East Harlem Performing Arts School). At fifteen, he traveled to Paris to perform in *Black & Blue*, a musical revue that later came to Broadway.

Savion appeared in the movie *Tap*, and played a dance teacher on Sesame Street for five years. At eighteen, he returned to Broadway in *Jelly's Last Jam*, performing with his mentor, Gregory Hines.

Savion loved to perform, but something was missing. He wasn't bringing his essence to the audience. He was dancing to someone else's beat. How could he be himself on stage?

The solution hit him one night at a hip-hop club. Why not tap to today's rhythms? Funk grooved through Savion, bopping round his body like a challenge to be met. He responded instantly, stomping out the feelings stirring up inside of him.

Tap meets hip-hop.

Savion finally knew how to express himself. And the chance came to do that when he choreographed and starred in a show revolving around his idea: "I want to bring in 'da noise, I want to bring in 'da funk."

On November 3, 1995, *Bring in 'da Noise, Bring in 'da Funk* opened at the Joseph Papp Public Theater in New York City.

On April 25, 1996, the show premiered on Broadway.

In *Bring in 'da Noise, Bring in 'da Funk*, Savion used tap and hip-hop to trace racism's roots—to which the origin of tap is linked. Slaves created rhythms to communicate with each other secretly when their drums were forbidden.

Portraying "'da Beat," Savion danced through some of history's darker moments. Tap was used as a kind of racial stereotyping in the early 1900s, when a grinning African-American tap dancer would perform for the amusement of white audiences.

The evolution of tap unfolded in the show as well, even as it showed a totally new concept of tap to the world. It was the first time hip-hop had ever found a home on "stuffy" Broadway. Savion's blending of tap and hip-hop changed the theater world.

Bring in 'da Noise, Bring in 'da Funk was a milestone for tap, and for Broadway. The theater world responded by presenting Savion with a Tony Award for best choreography.

Besides being possibly the greatest hoofer ever, Savion is widely credited for saving tap from obscurity. By uniting tap and hip-hop, he made hoofing "cool." He gave it new life and pushed it into its next phase.

BIBLIOGRAPHY

Glover, Savion & Weber, Bruce. *Savion!:
My Life in Tap.* New York: HarperCollins, 2000.

Laher, John. "King Tap: Savion Glover Moves a Tradition
into the Future." *New York Magazine*, October 22, 1995.

Vellela, Tony. "Broadway's Hot Teenage Tap Wonder:
Savion Glover." *The Christian Science Monitor*,
June 23, 1992.

To Casey and Michael, my boys who danced —S.C.

Thank you, Julia —L.F.

HOLIDAY HOUSE is registered in the U.S. Patent and Trademark Office.
Printed and bound in October 2022 at C&C Offset, Shenzhen, China.
The artwork was created with digital tools.
www.holidayhouse.com
First Edition
1 3 5 7 9 10 8 6 4 2

Library of Congress Cataloging-in-Publication Data
Names: Castrovilla, Selene, 1966– author. | Freeman, Laura (Illustrator),   illustrator.
Title: This is tap : Savion Glover finds his funk / by Selene Castrovilla; illustrated by Laura Freeman.
Description: First edition. | New York : Holiday House, 2023. | Includes bibliographical references.
Audience: Ages 4–8 | Audience: Grades K–1 | Summary: "An illustrated biography of Savion Glover,
tap dancer and choreographer, that shows how his love of music, dance, and self-expression as a young
boy sets him on the path to change how people see tap dancing"—Provided by publisher.
Identifiers: LCCN 2022007506 | ISBN 9780823438631 (hardcover)
Subjects: LCSH: Glover, Savion—Juvenile literature. | Dancers—United States—Biography—Juvenile literature.
Choreographers—United States—Biography—Juvenile literature. | Tap dancing—United States—History—Juvenile literature.
Classification: LCC GV1785.G56 C37 2023 | DDC 792.7/8092
[B]—dc23/eng/20220321
LC record available at https://lccn.loc.gov/2022007506

ISBN: 978-0-8234-3863-1 (hardcover)